Though the Walls Are Lit

THOUGH THE WALLS ARE LIT

Emily Holt

LOST HORSE PRESS
Sandpoint, Idaho

Acknowledgments

I am grateful to the editors of the following publications in which these poems first appeared:

The Best New British & Irish Poets (Eyewear, 2018): "Interface"
Brief Encounters: A Collection of Contemporary Nonfiction (W.W. Norton & Co., 2015): "Hunger"
Pontoon Poetry, "Impressionist"
Poetry Ireland Review: "Our Red Evening"
Talking River: "Interface"; in the sequence "On Your Anniversary . . .," the poem beginning "You wanted it clean . . ." and the poem beginning "Because I sleep through the night . . ."

I am also grateful to the editors of the 2019 Tomaž Šalamun Prize, the 2018 Tupelo Open Reading Period, the 2017 Patrick Kavanagh Award, and the Munster Literature Centre's 2016 Fool for Poetry Chapbook Competition, who commended previous versions and selected chapbooks of this manuscript, entitled *If Not Savior*. Sincere gratitude to Kevin Goodan and Kimberly Burwick for attentive readings of later drafts, and to Stan Sanvel Rubin and Judith Kitchen—for challenging me to take risks and for creating the Rainier Writing Workshop. For their generous teaching and mentoring, I would like to thank Fleda Brown, Rick Barot, and Sean McDowell. A special thank you to Samuel Green for making this seem possible. I am indebted to Paula Meehan and Theo Dorgan—for their poetry and for their hospitality in Dublin. I am grateful to Bernard, Grace, and Billie for their friendship and the many conversations that helped to create this book. For their hospitality in Northern Ireland and their willingness to share their stories, I would like to thank Mark Levine, Danny Morrison, Jack Duffin, DAZ, Niall, Zico, Makiko, Gerard, and the Bogside Artists—Tom and William Kelly and Kevin Hasson. For being my first home in Belfast, I would like to thank L'arche. I'm grateful to my father for teaching me to fill my life with music. This book would not be possible without family and friends both in the U.S. and in Ireland. Daily gratitude to Braden—for all the life off the page.

Cover Photograph: Braden Van Dragt.
Author Photo: Braden Van Dragt.
Book & Cover Design: Christine Holbert.

FIRST EDITION

This and other fine Lost Horse Press titles may be viewed online at www.losthorsepress.org.

LIBRARY OF CONGRESS CATALOGUING-IN-PUBLICATION DATA
Cataloguing-in-Publication Data may be obtained from the Library of Congress.
ISBN 978-0-9991994-9-7

For Eugenia O'Brien Tice
& Charlotte Kavanagh O'Brien
More than memory

& for Jean Ann Holt
My start and my finish

Table of Contents

The Preparation of the Body for Loss

To begin, I hear December

tender as a scalpel.
I stretch the canvas

ready the wine, the water.
In these modest rooms

I first licked the weapon—
Desire, yours, drifted

through the window,
and snow down the war.

When I tie the scarf
under my neck

I am her
and I am never

her   painting
that I may learn to hear the train

for something more precise—
a smattering of bullets

the buzzard's hiss and cry—
that I may wait

for my opaque pilgrim,
roped flesh to ghost

and ghost to flesh,
that I may receive

her mirror, her hands
poised behind the candle.

On Your Anniversary, in Lieu of a Mass, Reading of the 1981 Irish Hunger Strike

> While I wander in search of the dead,
> all I see are the living,
> being pulled into full existence
> emerging as if from a cellar.
>
> —Medbh McGuckian

I turn up the dial of my lipstick. To start, to give an account
of a time. No paper, just voices, snippets of song. I wet my lips
red, it wets the edge of the paper coffee cup I clutch as I sit, only
listening—

> *where the roadside bends,*
> *the roadside jam*
> *playin' on the edge of town—*

listening to the songs and what we call the news all rolling and
tucking together, mocking sense, mocking lines and right-angles

> [And I could sing but—]

but that in July I wrote in a thin tall notebook
on the way to the prison

> *When it's not always raining—*
> *Momma told me—*

She told me to stay
away   But today   it is all
that is left

These 3,000 images—
accountable only to the hurried streets
the numberless starlings

                                                    [And I could sing but—]

but the pallets stacked toward sky—
how inside each built ring lie not ruin
but the no longer useful bits of lives
old pillows   TVs   towels   books
as much life as the dead leave

                                                        So be not afraid
                                                           for I go—

I go toward a *you* and a *country*
built from silence and matches

                                                    I go before—

I throw the match   I start the music
& the unheard pages burn—

                                            [So I say to you—
                    If putting your hand to his face is your blood's doing
                                        not your hand's doing—]

Then Night   I coo to you
Come again no more—

Then Night   I tip easily into your arms
wanting   to be surrounded   by the orange of sodium lamps
wanting to wake   with senses dimmed

                                        Trust this body
                                        that says no pain
                                        will go to waste

for all about us is heat
summer heat   heat from the fires
circled by children   singing

Give me your hand   give me the fire—

Not mine up here   the streets   the alleys
The city takes you in   spits
tongues you with nicotine
South the fields say
come here child come here
you aren't seeing it right—the sea—
the sea   North   no letters
The silence keeps the pulse slow   cradles you
rocks you   North you sit off Botanic
sip instant   hear the city's three notes repeat
violin-lift   cane-hit on the drum
kitchen sink weeping

You must balance the meadow in the bottom right corner
with the smoke-drifts above   The trouble is the red—ruddy knees
obstinate hands   The canvas dips under their weight
Morning   boot-laces untied   drag and click   The boots
shuffle   No need to say whiskey won't be enough
He must balance the water within   calling   with night
the walk to Lough Neagh   the marches   through parts of town
If you were a mother   you'd want   to wall up the lake
stretch a row of razor-wire on top   *Mo cuisle*   you'd say

Mo cuisle   It is almost Easter   Wait for your wine
your deliverance   Go back to town   Watch your old alleys
fill-up with water   even if red watch it rise 'til it starts to glow
If you were a mother—but you are not   You only plan the walk
to the water   compose his funeral song at edge of violin   a broken bow
You'll take—*I was by hunger pressed*—and let it light up his face
You'll smoke it down   take it inside you   the way you want him there
walled beyond what prayer does   to the natural shape of hands

A thin man   sells clothing
at the market   The clothes never fit
The wine he drinks is over-sweet
More than one person will blame themselves
He's built of cell smoke   of words   the sort
you'd like to scream in mass   standing
on the pew   In the cell he circles
picks at the skin around his nails
He waits for a voice   In the white-walled
room a cassette player on a thin metal table
the tape plays his brother's voice
The cell is only locked from inside
When he wanders out on the streets   puts his ear
to the ground   to hear each layer
of dust   beer   blood   each crack in the concrete
is a tired mouth   smoke-whispering and still alive

He plays the same records over   and over
You grow a place in the mind   the pancake house
crowded   open all night   You ride the picture
to a garage   plastic crates   the record sleeve
in his hands   *Don't it make you want to not bother*
at all   But you've no child inside   and the lions
still scratching the den-walls   *15 families starving*
all around the corner block   because you have not
will not   leave this town   but keep the pilot light lit
Listen for your night-music   a fiddle jerking untuned
around high E   a mother's requests to stay in
the flute   a lover he's not seen in years
the bodhrán   boots wanting to dance   You haven't
the lover's fluid way of waving the hand   beckoning
and the song is in pieces   and you must ease it
with the drink   but 5 a.m. empty-handed
he comes in   still wearing each shot 'round the neck
the camera-strap growing rusty   his hands
holding each shot he did not take   the mother's
mute wandering   the couple's wet cigarettes
at the check-point   milk bottles tossed
blue glass at the barricade

Target over the eye
Can't see the red
dot but see him

The train goes on
Each window a face
I sip   from the car's wind

The platform dew-
soaked   The photographer's hair
wet   just out of the shower

Board the train and his fingers
clench   Stay and he'll go
to his next job   Stay

and I'll learn to paint
something other than moon-
faces in rubble   white flags

in the wrong hands   Stay
and your brother will scratch
one more line in the row

To think we met here
Thrashed by mid-
day sun   Our lost

ones asleep in us
Lungs full and the
nights not yet butcher-

blocks   Our beds made
and dry and wanting

Wire-darkened   The Bible whole and indifferent
in the corner   A room   and not a room   A cell
You took your time to get the light just so   2 a.m.
and visions rise   red pills crawl along the windowsill
4 walls   or is it 6? 10? a hall? a row?
Disinfectant sprayed at the lip of the door
Or lips gone to wine   The walls shifting   Inner
and outer   the men are heaving   their hands are stained
with shit-petals   or blood   their names a blur
'til the *Hands up arms out*   though you want to say
My brother   my brother is coming   see him coming?

Gone the cell   Silent the water   dead grey   its white
spray   Gone   the city too still   Still the cells   still
the going   She walks alleys looking   for him
whether walled or under the skin   Within each   an abyss
Alleys spinning red   grey   *Will you have a drink?*
Will you have me? Here   the wet alleys   Here the hotels
targets   If he ever comes back   his wool coat   the boots
unlaced outside the shower   Wash the skin off   wash
the prison off   Soak   look out   your arms an extension
of the railings   the thin balconies   unaccountable
to the river   Know where you are   Here   No where
No place the dead won't go   won't reach for
the way the skin of one body   roughened with sweat
will   or won't   reach for another

When you take to him   shadows on the walls   galvanized
metal sipping at the light   You've been there before
an empty room   electricity out   a wool blanket on the floor
Though it's July   a shudder in the air   the only fire
outside   up the street   bred of tires   stacked
that poor man's monument   fence posts
and diaper boxes and chair legs and bedposts
and headboards and who even has all of that to spare
You stay up all night   sleep a prayer   An avenue
of fog light up to the corner   The shots are louder
and the holes between the houses swallow boys
with notes shoved down their trousers   Mud-covered boots sit
by the door and a mother shakes   her head   'til her bones are still

I want to swallow   this drink he's made
so I take another sip—
orange dots my vision   He leans and asks me
to repeat myself   this man   only doing
his duty   If I take another sip
the wall out back   will still be marked
He asks me to repeat myself
Who will feed the dog tomorrow?
The wall out back will still be marked
A line of razor-wire on top won't do
I ask   *Who will feed the dog tomorrow?*
His hands rest nicely on the table
nails trimmed   even if red 'round the edges
A line of razor-wire won't do   Here   There
Orange dots my vision   He leans closer
His hand presses mine nicely to the kitchen table
I want to swallow this drink he's made

You know you only fear   the death you've held
the one you've touched   the breath you've lost
the way struggling to breathe can turn your mind around
When you woke in the night too far from the hospital
and your mother drove through the night   ash branches
sketching the night   and the doctors put you in front
of that white screen to capture your lungs or your throat
tightening   you wondered why bones would be the point
nothing crushed or broken   no fall
But the inkling that the bones might be the point
As an adult you learned how a camera works
you learned what else an x-ray can show or at least
insinuate   and every time a shutter clicked
you felt as though standing before you was a boy
short-haired   eyes blue at the seams
standing in a gown open at the back

Going to the field for you   (& blue beside the grey)
starlings pass & bricks rise   sex the cause of it   Durex the sheath—
Your hands smell of gelignite and her   The night hard on her mouth
Holding the mare for you   holding the woman for you
her wrists under my hands   Faces dwindle in the mirror
(& blue beside the grey)   I survive the lamplight
the muttering inside on the telephone   & the back-shot of snow
You will not let them forget it is winter   This mother will forget
the red she made and the white against   You will dodge the cells
And I your hand   The bed between us growing

The hard edge of waking
face-down   paint brushes drying
on the windowsill above my head
House quiet   I seep into the sheets
stomach-first   House quiet but for a cough
Granny   A chair at the kitchen table
scoots   drags dust
'Sí do mhaimeo í   'sí do mhaimeo í
The hag with the money   coughs
She is   one breath   another
She is waking
Today   she is my waking
I can't name
the particular birds then
But still   the song—
Late enough for summer
and so drink haunting tongue
I should have said
I will let you down properly
your body lowering   as I am laid
low   but blue pills collecting in the cup
wind snapping sheets on the line
In a few hours or a few
minutes   who can tell   I'll want
to wrap myself in a corner of this box
this room   this cell   It's just a room
I want my skin smoother as yours
is smooth   I can't even tell which man
I mean   I've my father's two working hands
but no work and breasts
here to usher no one in   We know
I'd tear them up   anyone who dared
follow   Razors dance   jig along
the windowsill   The shade won't keep them out
Or the sun   Partial and wintering

When you step into shade—

In a strange bed   I rise
with grey   with blue

He sits before fence-screen
and razor-wire   listens
for the return   his brother's boots

When you step into shade, step down

In our strange bed   this blue shuddering
wipes clean   the voice that asks

But aren't we strangers still?

The automatic blinds are broken
& naked   you   crouching in the dark
are a blue storm at my door
Rain lights the frame the color of linoleum
you kneel on   relying only   on the pleasure of sight
my ante   already on the table   a bruised thigh
a cigarette laid down   my December asks
On the street below   the bridge
falls   the song falters   Through it all
the others sleep   unwilling
to make of their arms a sheet flown up
a naked man crouching   a fiddle player eying all that's cut him
any body willing to touch silence   to disarm

Silence revolves   our mouths   on the mattress
on the ground   The ground takes care of things   I rise
take the sheets like cling-wrap   Let's preserve this
Let's forget this   There's a force 10 gale outside
There's a crack under the door   Our questions dangle
like used pay phones   I offer to find a home
for his blue razor   But *he* becomes *you*
And you offer   the blood on your hand
Outside   whole trees are in motion

Tonight there is some boy dying
of something innocent   The streets
redden   the buses lit with hands
incarnadine   grave-restive

Tonight the boy's mother will hold
her hands   I did not see you before
you went   though my name on your lips
was a window   open   high on a cell wall

high and smelling of hawthorn
I don't know why the lamps
will not redden   The television is bound
to the floor and we to it

Our hands are still free
Their children smile for new shoes
and thank their jailor   feel Nothing—*nothing*
he says   *She feels nothing*   He wants to know

how to say that   I tell him the children
draw emptiness in the colors
the TV selects   when some mother's son
dies in the back of a car

I tell him   when they reach inside me
the red will not be pure or shine
So suffer tonight my thirst
There are miles of men before

So let me be the riot   shifting through your hands
Know nothing can come of it
Know I chose the knife to reap
to cut me to a side of the city   you won't pass through safely

You with the blood
over your eye   the burnt
hair   Take this cup
of water   drink it

all at once   breathing
the off-gulps
Leave him out of it
He hasn't enough time

The car is wrecked
the seats shimmering
and you   all sinew
and devilment   glass

in your hair   When you walk
home tonight   walk on
the left   Let the
passersby—all two or

three of them—let
their headlights light your
head   Let them see

the cut glowing   your
eyes dead-on   They
will not know you
They will see their

own   heading home
the last time   Let
them have that

The door will not stay shut
                    You left
the sheets the way they were

No priest at the door   just the dumb
phone swinging   Tonight
you will navigate the crowds

the rioting will hold you both   each step

closer   to the snow and flame of his wrist
    the sky   raw   livid   opening

Because I sleep through the night
I name the dead by morning
I am not without blame
It is a list that takes no paper
It takes all the time we're trying to kill
when the sun turns
Even if I had six shopping bags full
of pen and cigarette paper
the Mountain Climber and the Angel
to guide me to the cell
the bodies would still crowd up
on the heating pipes
and from that hour to this
those that can suffer the most
will feed each other by force

I wake and your brother says war
war ships on the water
we sleep above
But it's been ages since
the clothing issue
those epic fasts
When I find him I find you
and don't know how to turn
to them   Each ship and rubber
and ounce of weed killer   each gun
each inside the other   and all the other
words that spin   each feeding
each other at the breast
though the mother is hemorrhaging
and the walls are lit   are
tongued with meadow orchids

You wanted it to be clean   as nothing
is clean   you wanted car   peeler   bomb
even   though all are red brown grey   night
underneath   You wanted it to fit
with the city's score   the bodies on the screen
in the papers   You wanted—

nothing wet   or cold   nothing sharp
or singular   no wine taken   no pills
swallowed   *More than one person*
will blame themselves   You wanted
barricades   not water   not wrist cut
not breath leaving   not his final and only

and utter memory of light and arms holding
his final and only and utter *Oh*—

For Those Minutes North,
This Hour Through the South of Me

> Arklow is a very unremarkable town.
> It's a town on the way to somewhere else.
>
> —*Sam Smyth*

I side-step the white coats because *wound*

                              —how it opens.

And each office has become one, the hours distilled,
      and the drink is fine.

                         Such issues are often caused

—the doctors, the specialists circle—

                         by misuse, repeated injury, trauma.

I smile a bit, try to think of an *inciting incident* in the past 6 months
      or so—

                              they make steady eye contact
                                        and ask

      because a rib strung to my spine is out of place.

      because my jaw is misaligned. Keeps locking shut.

      because the cells in my womb might be off, stuck to each
            other the wrong way.

Because I'll take that song in Irish and up the ante—
going through the south of me
I've a wound where others have a home.

They do not come out with it.

And my mind is a grey fog on a tight, red alley. A sore alley.

Sore because I've just been in Belfast.
Because nothing happened in Belfast,
nothing to cause these wounds,
as far as I can tell.

Their eyes say I've played a part.

They ask: *Are you safe?*

I allow: *You're years too late.*

It wasn't just one place.

[And I could sing but—]

But I remember July
fit to burst—
the strain of her hands not here.
Here another language, and leaves
another color and wind

burrowing to the pit of me—

Still, the telephone rings:
the dahlias are burning
are ready for mass—

And standing before the congregation
I say nothing of my desire
that darkening wind

I could say,
The anniversary of my birth
We burned candles in her bed—

                                        [And I could sing but—

But there is no singing
of her starvation
that fatal pregnancy

                                        but the blood
                        running along a bone born out of place]

There is no singing
Though yes, I admit, yes—

We were still ravenous.

                                        [Oh how the blood there
                                            is brighter—]

Our Red Evening

Part of every dream, the train, loud, lunatic,
lifts a din of rail and rim through Greystones, Bray.

The sea—a net—sways and wraps
the evening in mist. Faces frost the window.

One woman up the coast, another down.
Sunset, and skin pales, glows. Is sheer.

No blood on the hospital sheets—
all in her head—and you bloodshot now

on the train. Gone Dún Laoghaire, still
Rathdrum, Arklow—the train marks each exile

with a sign. But exile—how it sleeps now
in your mother's hair. What you put inside

you can't take back. So bí i do thost, child.
Let the silhouette of south hill on sea take you back

to water. Here, take a glass, a cup. Drink
your mother back. Drink your town back,

that town of men bent on hill-walking, wrist
-clawing, senseless straying. Gone you

knew it still lived in your bone. Your own
daughter waits in the city. One woman,

another. The line of you will stretch—
You will walk together down the coast—

hair down, you will walk in white shifts your mothers made.

Now and at the Hour

When she began
Death, I began to kill

the mice. The first
by trap, the last

by hand. Her pain
was slow, one said.

She became *They*
in the cigarette mouths

we pay to usher
The Great Undying

down that long path
strewn with dinner plates.

Rust-reared and penitent,
I pushed Them aside,

knelt my grim mystery down.
I push them, still,

like mice.

Arklow, my garden, my grave
the streets—

but the word
how it paints   how it waits
for ship   for guard   for execution

                              [And I could sing but—
                                only this kind of body
                            can have water break from it]

In the language you use everyday
maybe you'd say, *your own* language
oh how the arms tire—

Streets of Arklow

I come for the song, the sound running
all down my life, all tin-whistle and vocal-note,
streetlight and dusk on Main Street,
the song an intimacy fit for three,
one in a long white dress,
faces as if they've remade communion
and received it in the dunes by the sea,
rising with fog on their shoulders, on their lips,
orange, resting like tongues.
When I returned, if not savior
then supplicant, I knew your face
would jacket me again. This town
where all I can do is kneel at grave, at pew,
at the storm of hands, never so desired,
so blue, but here where night
touches town and moans, eager
for morning—hazed with violence,
and red underneath, a crack in the sun.

Hunger

Arklow, An tInbhear Mór, The Great Estuary

One never manages to determine the instant
when a stimulus once seen is seen no longer.

—Maurice Merleau-Ponty

Arklow—the beautiful word conceals, starting as it does with the soft *a* and ending open, evoking the bows of fiddle strings, windows to the sea.

Arklow—the squat white and pink houses at the edge of the prisoner's window. He's lined up pills on the windowsill. Not yet awake, he thinks he'll rise and see the sea, knowing, knowing it's only the river Avoca, *smothered river, battle-worn river, the meeting of the waters.*

Arklow—all word and image, but here, they're not the same. The language is in the mind, but the mind paints, used to telling itself a good story, waiting for the ship, the guard, the execution.

Image—what but memory? The moment before light enters the eye, we hope to be astonished, lie and say we want pattern.

Public—the white gothic arches of Shelton Abbey where prisoners raise cattle for Africa; a vale of two lakes, the one always hidden in fog; the pottery shop at the bottom of the town; men smoking in the old shipyard, huddled and cursing the coalfish, the rockling, the bare waters.

Private—the house on Main Street, Arklow, February 1996. Into the ceasefire, and does that matter here, where a child peers past a wisp of white hair to an ice-water bath? Does it matter when, still, there's the sense one could be made to freeze or drown, any minute? Door open to the yard, the smell of turf saying *Return*. Not *Go back* but *Come back*. Gate open to a street of 32 pubs. Our pub—Kitty's, where the children go too. Beyond, the hills, the Wicklow Mountains. The Mottie Stone. Back down in the valley, The Orchard, blood in the lambing sheds. Beds that dip in the middle. A mother stationed in an armchair by a false fireplace. She announces to the room, 'The hall-door is crooked.' *Crooked*, she says, insistent. *Sober*, she says. Insistent, the sibilant *s* and clatter of *t*, the sounds of a scold, wind in silver firs.

Here, in Arklow, sound is everything, each word a veil for a thing too-fragile, raw at the edges. The session, the screaming. A drunken cousin cooing "Hush Little Baby," rocking the two-year-old niece she just met. Inventing lyrics that turn dirty, echo the grunts in the driveway below. A child whose mother, and father, will leave her. Others say, *drink, bipolar*. We're up to date, though our patterns persist. Headlights flash on the cemetery, below, where, if I lived here, I would be buried. The sound of a heel slipping on concrete, a gasp. Guttural. No sense to it. Rubbish.

Still, we're flush with speech. We try to choose, sort *illness* and *prison* from *come* and *yes*, cut *wait* from *leave*, listen for the unsaid edge: *suicide*. One that rises like bile, like whiskey, swiftly and inevitably. Act or accident? Climbing over a fence, a man leans on a gun. Where's the logic, the movement? Where are the wooden fences, in this country of wire? Where did the bullet enter? Hand, rib, stomach? Could he still feel his hunger then? Past and present, *hunger* infuses it all. Bread dipped in tea, beer batter licked off paper. Sexual hunger. Spiritual hunger. No specific word for satiation. Just, *Come back, please, come back*. Here, it's never just one place. Each one gnaws at your hand. Exile is built-in, desired as much as required. We're indirect, all possibilities running off in rivers that splinter the country, because who would want to choose just one river?

One river means one house means one cell means one grave. So many ways, so many rooms to keep passion from spilling over the walls. If river is town is prison, do we enter it to slow the suicide? Do we wear the town to slow the desire? Images cascade, converge, fall apart. And I'm left with one human life tucked away in the pubs, the shops, the petrol station. Arklow. Two housing estates divided by a field. A dumpster at the edge. Footprints that round out where green metal feet rise from the mud. Round marks—where knees could go.

Fever Dream

Childless in Arklow we lay by the blue-black river,
California a hymn for tired lips,
no hint of that long, grey winter.

Here in California, winter hills sea-green, the sea a shiver
down the coast—it's all a cruel light-trick.
Child, take me back to lie by the blue-black river.

In California, we lose what we make, one life briefer
than dew. Child, you'd never believe the blue silk
dress, your father's hands before that grey winter.

Take me back to the transistor radio, a quiver
of song, no money in our pockets and no curled fist.
Childless and proud, we lay by the blue-black river.

There's no thunder in me now, daughter,
your face nearly lost in the sick-room mist.
Childless once, we lay by the blue-black river.
Nothing to outlive us but that tireless winter.

The Door

after Adam Zagajewski

She is not yet gone
The moon crawls past
A child trips on her gown

The doctor in his car listens to John Lee
(waiting, waiting on the waterfront)
She is not yet gone

How dreadful
There is still so much to eat
and the grass rained on

The streets brighter than before
She is not yet gone
(Though blessed is the fruit—)

Blessed is a whole part of me
already away with her
living through the sane moments

My garden, my grave,
streets of Golgotha, be not afraid—

                              [be not this body, given up—]

                       [But what—what if you let me be—]

not so much to be consoled, not so much
to drink, as to know, not so much a roof

as a mother, as bread, as the two-at-onceness of hunger,
of want, the here and there of it. Let me walk

left of the wall, by the hedges at night.

                           [Oh I could sing but—]

The roads will remain empty,
no one's feet
but your own, echoing in the shop
boarded up for the night

Waiting for God

after the writings of Simone Weil

The fishing village wretched
on the feast day of its patron saint.
The wives in procession,
holding candles and singing ancient hymns,
like the song of boatman on the Volga—

I cannot help belonging
though indistinguishable to the eye
from the pale walls washed with lime.
The full moon over the sea,
a mark on my forehead.
The women's hands, their candles—
nothing brutal.
I had forgotten my past.

Ever since you were a child,
you tried to get there,
the sea full by the moon, the candles,
the ashes on your forehead.
But once you got there—
how different it was.
The village open,
the soldiers arriving at night.

Visitation

I dream mostly of labor
an old greased hospital
where labor was nothing
much to speak of.

At 8 cm, I am sent back
to a time when Hunger stalked each bog
and asphodel. The custom then,
when the mother died,

was to fasten the door.
Shrouded in blood-sheet and shadow
I receive the child on my chest
for a moment short as morning.

I tell her we are from a land
where God was smug
and fat (And still it is so).
I tell her that tomorrow

we will check the grave,
make sure it is clean.
We lay by an open door
in rough-clover and sea-kale and heath dog-violet
until I know the child is gone

with the mountains and wood-rushes.
It is so much the better.
The grass here barely blows.

Plea

for the child of cockcrow & sunup   for a future in which I learn
    to hear blood
& the moon   in which I bend to paper

the way I bent to sweep hairs
from her forehead   from the ground I've built for her—

caustic   astral   subordinate to water
& floating mirrors   to hands pressed to knees—

To a future in which I no longer say
Opaque pilgrim,
let me follow—

I See Her Face in the Train Window

And what could He send to match the human
Fact of waiting, weak, for that opaque pilgrim,
Mercy? Each day I raise the voices of my dead,

Roped flesh to ghost and ghost to flesh.
I say, *Lord, grant me an hour of death*
Amongst women. And He may listen.

I say, *Grant me a listening with,* not *for.*
And He may listen.
But after this, she is still our exile.

And after this she is still gone—
So *bí i do thost.* Let the silhouette of south
Hill on sea take you back. Let that yoke

Of wet and light that stretches up the coast
Teem down. Hear the Mother's voice,
Thou my best thought, thou my true light,

O hear me—
I am not yet gone.

And my hands still, though the day is sun,
And my body taken beyond all women,

Beyond the old unwavering dreams,
Beyond this quiet sleep-work,
The wrench and chisel of each day after.

Interface

She is always there   the woman
with the plastic mask   on the wall

of the museum   and before that
I'd assume   in the paper the week

the bomb went off   and I wonder
maybe even now   sitting through her own

life   Or sanctum   bending
to a granddaughter in a crib   Does she still

wear the mask   I wonder   or was it meant only
for the healing   for the aftermath   the camera?

I wonder   and yet   I find   her face is searchable
the engine numb under my fingers

her life the subject of articles because the issue
of compensation is unresolved and her case—

shrapnel still in her neck and children to feed—
one of the more difficult   you could say

I do say   though now I'm measuring
Lives surely call   for the measuring stick

a wall of distinction   between here and there
a face with scars   and a hand   scarred   a hand striking   and a face

struck by light   too early in the morning

Only to Paint a Cross

Is nothing   the pelvic bone

Untouched   no memory-bruise
Or crimson divination

Of birth   I turn from her voice
Intimate of branches

And magpies   Her only sin
Disappointment

The body now
A series of letters

Empty hands are nothing
to the living—

So give me the summer
I tiptoed night

To the yellow room
Give me the summer-night room

Give me a last breath
Do not give me hawkbit
   ragwort   rock-rose

Only give me
            yellow

Impressionist

One morning we ran out of black
and thought *birth*   rather than *stop*   or *loss*

Night before   supposed to go
for cadmium and ochre   but the women

and their movement with wine   nothing
we could capture   if that was the point all along

object-makers or subject-painters
it is always about abeyance

Because speech would not obey him
wheat fields with ravens   the potato eaters

eventually the razor to the ear   and the cold white bed
White being the absence of all   why did we ever want

it here where no image   is innocent
It's the question of why I want only to watch you here

with the light   on the left side of your head   here in my doorway
where we can't remember the contours of hands—

I'd raise the brush but colors   in their craving
all hot and holy   lift   like hymns   song razed

to ceiling   to the paint-flecked bedposts   the fire in them still
fire lighting our great opal sky   an attempt—

I'm breaking down   but the canvas   still   joining hands
and the river outside   still and listening

The Yarragh

> You have to have the yarragh in your voice.
>
> —*John McCormack*

You couldn't call it clean
this voice I carry   harmonica mixed in
with the vocal notes   the sounds
of an unremarkable town
They are harder to hear
mornings I must arrange the flowers
I do not know their name   but want
to give you the sense of touch
so I'll say cranberry and gorse
though I know there was a rose

I need it most   mornings the priest is teetering
his coffee mugs and piled newspapers
waiting for me   his hands
unfamiliar with true deliverance
with rough apparitions
the world given to her   in the hands
of a man's eyes   the salt-spray
of waves on her thighs   the summer spray
on shore   and the sprigs of black mountain heath

I need it most   mornings you are teetering
between here and there   and you've got me
there with you   on a street in a town
we both know is gone   or running
from a single bed in a cell   from betting slips
and hunger swallowing more than air
from your hand tense between edge
and center of *Veedon Fleece   St. Dominic's Preview*

51

Into the Music   where it's fine to say we're
lifted up again by the Lord   because we know
the word is more space than being

This voice is a note   so unquenched
and fugitive   even hunger can't catch it
It may not be the most articulate
but it comes from one of those streets
Lead Belly and skiffle   just Mahalia Jackson
and Lonnie Donnegan singing good morning
like blue was the only color worth painting
the only color worth your father's Friday pay

Still This Thirst

You're supposed to mourn a certain way   supposed
to draw a circle around it   fill it in   opaque   no cross

-hatching   Take the man I live with   take this   yellow
house at the edge of town   There is no circle here

I peer through both   I see milk crates of old records
I see his brother's camera   Some days   to appease those outside

these stucco white walls   I call Jon *his brother*
I let them have that distance   I think it means they'll look away

be relieved   thank me   Yes   It means I can draw broken
lines off the page   cross-hatch where I like   let silence stand in

for the good work of grieving   with an end in mind
I coach others on how to find this end   but I want

I want his T.B. Sheets   I want
something to touch   I want *the cool room   the fool's room*

I want to open the window   and breathe—

But we know better   You don't visit the town of the dead
You don't paint it   The light's never right

You learn to hear doors shifting
through cracks in a roof   for voices

that would end the search
that craving for fixed shelter   how it gets mixed up

with the urge to drink   colors your vision

So we go to the water   drive west from the rows
of house and park and dairy farm   to find that sharper

salt-air smell   the beach littered with seaweed
the shape of a hand   lost at sea

Even in this drought   there's water
on our tongues   on words that end

arbitrarily   We think   we think it random   Until they form

the names   of our   of your dead   and then
how they stretch   unbroken   off the page

your lips   We drink   in drought   We drink and drink

To Thee Do I Come

December and other months
to cleanse. Cedar-bodies
to sway. Remember Cyprus Avenue?
Child-like in our suede coats
fur boots, us all light-
strings, you with your camera
Why bother with drink
or bleeding when neither
are a sign of what's to come?
I will listen. I will listen
and you will search each crease
in your hand, and I shall see the rubble
for the house and the wanting
shall be enough

Notes & Translations

Page 5: The McGuckian epigraph is from "Life as a Literary Convict" in *The Soldiers of Years II* (Wake Forest University Press, 2002).

The italicized lines are from Van Morrison's "Ancient Highway" and "Days Like This," *Days Like This* (1995). Reprinted with permission of the artist and BMG.

Page 6: The line "*Come again no more*" echoes the American folk tune, "Hard Times Come Again No More," Stephen Foster, 1854.

The interlude evokes language in the Catholic *Liturgy of the Eucharist* and from the hymn, "Be Not Afraid," Bob Dufford, S.J., 1973.

Page 7: The line, "*Give me the fire*" is a refrain from "Ancient Highway," and "Give me your hand" is the Anglicized title of the traditional Irish song "Tabhair dom do Lámh," 17th century, Ruaidri Dáll Ó Catháin, (c.1570-c.1650)

Page 9: *Mo cuisle* is Irish for *my pulse*. The italicized lines are from the 1870s folk song "Paddy's Lamentation."

Page 11: The italicized lines are from Morrison's "The Great Deception," *Hard Nose the Highway* (1973), and from "Not Supposed to Break Down," *The Philosopher's Stone* (1998). Reprinted with permission of the artist and Warner Chappell Music.

Page 19: The italicized phrases '*Sí do mhaimeo í* refer to a *sean-nós* song from Connemara.

Page 31: Sam Smyth's quote is from a documentary about Van Morrison, *Van Morrison Under Review: 1964-1974.*

Page 34: The phrase, *bí i do thost,* is Irish for *shh,* or "bit of quiet."

Page 37: "Streets of Arklow" is also the title of a song from Morrison's *Veedon Fleece* (1974).

Pg. 38: The epigraph is from Maurice Merleau-Ponty, *The Phenomenology of Perception* (Routledge, 2002) p. 6.

Page 42: Repeated lines in "The Door" (and page 47, "I See Her Face...") riff off Louis MacNeice's "Prayer Before Birth," *Collected Poems: Louis MacNeice* Wake (Forest University Press, 2013), p. 213.

Page 44: The scene draws from Simone Weil's description in *Waiting on God*, translated by Emma Craufurd, G.P. (Putnam's Sons, 1951).

Page 47: "Thou my best thought . . ." references an Irish hymn, "Be Thou My Vision," commonly attributed to St. Dallán Forgaill (c. 530-598).

Page 51: The quote from John McCormack comes from the 1930 film, *Song O' My Heart*, directed by Frank Borzage, distributed by Fox Film Corporation.

The lines "rough apparitions / the world given to her / in the hands / of a man's eyes" draw on Hélène Cixous's "Savoir" from *Veils*, translated by Geoffrey Bennington (Stanford University Press, 2001).

The phrase "lifted up again by the Lord" echoes a line in Morrison's "Full Force Gale" from *Into the Music* (1979). Reprinted with permission of the artist.

Page 53: Italicized lines are drawn from Morrison's "T.B. Sheets," *Blowin' Your Mind!* (1967). Reprinted with permission of the artist and Universal Music Publishing Group.